Weekly Wins

52 Essential Lessons to Make Your
Real Estate Business Flourish

ROLAND KYM

Weekly Wins: 52 Essential Lessons to Make Your Real Estate Business Flourish

Copyright © 2017 by Roland Kym

ISBN 978-1548899516

Printed in USA and Canada

To my wife and children
who will always be my driving force.

Contents

By Week

By Categories
Starting Out

Self Management

Foreword

by

Marvin Alexander

I first met Roland when he approached Keller Williams Canada to discuss opening the first Keller Williams market center in Vancouver, BC. Most people don't know that by agent count KW is the largest real estate franchise in the world with well over 115,000 agents at that time, and in 2017 more than 170,000 agents call Keller Williams home. That's a lot of family members to remember, so when one of them sticks out in your mind you know they have to be special.

At the time, I had a track record of success, previously being the #1 Realtor in Canada and other agents were watching me. None more than Roland, but he always took every piece of advice to heart, not just from me, but everyone, showing a thirst for learning and growing and a talent for reducing things to their essentials and getting more bang for his buck than others. He also had an incredible work ethic and it wasn't long before I noticed his name swiftly climbing the ranks in sales. Yet, I also knew by reputation that he was one of the straight shooters who everyone enjoyed working with and had really balanced his life well.

Roland isn't stuck on presenting a fancy image or big status, he actually does what he sets out to achieve and no less.

It doesn't surprise me that Roland's book, *Weekly Wins,* has effectively taken the complexities of the real estate industry and life balance and simplified them into a logical, concise and easy to read book that should serve as a handbook for all business people, not just Realtors.

If you are a new agent or a seasoned one you need to learn, relearn and refresh your skills into habits. Roland's bite-sized lessons and Actions Steps format will help you do this, and I am sure that smart agents will find that after a year their copy will be a dog-eared book that they wouldn't be without.

Well done for giving us *Weekly Wins* Roland!

Marvin Alexander
Director of Keller Williams Canada Realty
Previously ranked as the #1 Realtor® in Canada, and #1 Realtor® for Keller Williams World Wide

A Word From a New Agent

I started as an administrative assistant, and as I now begin my own career in Real Estate I feel incredibly fortunate to have Roland as a mentor. As a new agent, I appreciated Roland's honest and straight-forward approach to achieving success and maintaining his values in such a complex business. For those starting out in such a competitive business, who may lack the confidence of an experienced Realtor, *Weekly Wins* is a fantastic resource. It can be easy to lose sight of your core values and goals but Roland's insight into overcoming challenges, how he treats clients and colleagues, or just tackling daily hurdles comes back to his core beliefs which are inspiring and beneficial to all.

He has made me look forward to my own Realtor career with confidence.

Caitlin Eyles
New Realtor

Introduction

The reason I'm in the top 2% of all Realtors is that my clients, who understand real estate, know that I'm always looking out for their best interests. I'm highly skilled in analyzing buildings and market trends and macro/micro market factors, but that's not enough. A great agent's role is no longer to find the listings, but to save clients time and money by figuring out the best possible deal at that time. Even then, a great agent may not reach their potential if they don't apply good business habits and implement key changes to how they operate in the world.

This book is the result of journaling my real estate experiences over the years. Journaling has been a valuable way of learning from my past experiences. I often felt at times that being a Realtor can be a very lonely profession made better if you share your experiences with other people. The potential of *Weekly Wins* is for an individual Realtor to read my lessons, learn from my experiences and reflect on what they did, or would do in similar situations. In this way, they will realize that they are not alone in their experiences. The Good, the Bad and the Strange situations in real estate are experienced by most top realtors.

You also have an opportunity to use *Weekly Wins* as a team. Your office or brokerage can create a learning seminar from the 52 lessons. Have a Realtor lead a session where they discuss my lessons, share their own experiences and review my action steps. Participants can openly discuss the challenges they have encountered and create actions steps the group suggests. In this way the team would be creating their own best practice action steps for each of the lessons that *Weekly Wins* discusses.

The purpose of this book is to create an experience-based resource that most Realtors can draw value from. The lessons are insights gained from my successes and failures which I've put into five key categories:

1. Starting Out
2. Self Management
3. Winning Customer Service
4. Winning Business Practices
5. Dealing with Challenges

Starting Out lessons are about rookie mistakes that even many experienced real estate agents, though no longer rookies, still make. These lessons are recommended best practices for those that are either starting out or those that want to start again.

Self Management is about the discipline we have to instill in ourselves to make successful habits and attitudes second nature.

Winning Customer Service is just that, the big and little things that are both behind the scenes and in front, that directly contribute to our customer's satisfaction.

Winning Business Practices are my practices that can strengthen any business, real estate or otherwise.

Dealing with Challenges provides guidance on what to do when things go sideways, because they can always go sideways.

Sometimes we get caught up in the doing of tasks and ignore the planning, analysis and skill-building that will propel us to the next level. We then wonder why we aren't moving forward personally and professionally. This book will help you take that first step in elevating your business to that next level.

My sincere wish is that you pick up this book weekly to inspire you to build a better real estate business over the next year. You can read the book by categories or discover them as you cycle through the 52 weeks of lessons. By living the lessons, my business continues to flourish and I want yours to flourish too.

Roland Kym
CEO
RolandKym.com

> *"Just as your car runs more smoothly and requires less energy to go faster and farther when the wheels are in perfect alignment, you perform better when your thoughts, feelings, emotions, goals and values are in balance."*

Brian Tracy
World Renowned Sales and Performance Expert

STARTING OUT

Core Values

Knowing and following your core values gives you focus and direction. My four core business values are:

1. I always look out for my client's best interest, whether a transaction takes one month or one year. The relationship carries on beyond a transaction and I continue to look out for their best interests. This is the foundation of my relationship with them.

2. I use innovative marketing and promotional tools to sell my listings.

3. I develop systems and use technology to ensure that all my clients receive the same top level of customer service and an excellent end result.

4. I work harder and smarter than most people and nothing I've learned over the years will ever replace hard work.

ACTION STEPS

Take some time and ask yourself, *what are my core values? What is most important that I want to hold myself accountable to? What do I want to be known for?* Core values are the pillars of your business that you model your business around.

1. Write down your core values.
2. Print them off and keep them in sight.
3. Stay true to them.

"Only as you do know yourself can your brain serve you as a sharp and efficient tool. Know your own failings, passions, and prejudices so you can separate them from what you see."

Bernard Baruch
Wall Street Legend

SELF MANAGEMENT

Know Yourself
Reflect vs. React

Know who you are and how you typically react to situations. For example, I know that I'm an honest, hard-working, yee-haw! cowboy who wants to solve everything instantly. As a Realtor, there are a dozen issues at any moment needing your attention. I've made mistakes by responding too quickly to situations that arise, only to learn that there were better ways of responding later. This approach of trying to quickly solve the problem caused me more issues and created more work later. It would have been much wiser and I would have had better results if I had taken some time to reflect before responding, or asked for advice.

As an example, I tried to solve a problem that a client thought may be a major barrier to her buying which was additional parking. I did all kinds of research in the area trying to resolve this, but it turned out that it was just a difficult parking area.

Later, I found out two things; firstly, a colleague let me know of upcoming changes to parking regulations that only a few people knew about, so I wish I had asked her at the start.

Secondly, I found parking wasn't so much an issue with the client herself as with her daughter who wasn't going to live with her and rarely visited. Had I gathered more information from the client initially, I could have effectively managed her objection sooner, but I rushed to "fix it" instead.

Know yourself, manage your strengths and weaknesses and ultimately use what is appropriate for the situation.

ACTION STEPS

1. Learn to understand your personality traits and how you typically react. Your natural instincts are valuable, however not in all situations. List any typical responses you have when difficult situations arise.

2. After reflection, list possible new ways of reacting. Learn how other people respond to situations that may work better. Begin to grow your skill set even if it feels uncomfortable.

3. Start building a sphere of trusted people around you. Take situations that you are dealing with to them and accept their advice on how to respond to heart.

I've found that these simple steps have broadened my perspectives and allowed me to become a better orchestrator of my life. As a result, I've now learned to block my first impulse and reflect before I respond. Are there other typical reactions you take that hold you back? Be honest and take the action steps above to improve these reactions.

> *"Your most unhappy customers are your greatest source of learning."*

> **Bill Gates**

WINNING CUSTOMER SERVICE

Turn Unhappy Customers Into Happy Ones

I recently treated myself to a foot massage which was my indulgence after an intense week. I decided to try a massage outlet that is a sister location to the one that I enjoy near home. Rather than being the relaxing experience I was used to, this visit started off on a sour note. I had to wait 45 minutes until they had time for me. The masseuse continuously flipped through his cell phone, essentially giving me a one-handed massage. I endured this sub-par service for 15 minutes before I stood up and said I couldn't participate in it any further.

I spoke with the receptionist about it and she offered to give me to another masseuse right away, but I was already running late my next appointment. I wasn't offered another opportunity for a different time or day. In the end, I left an unhappy customer and they lost my future business. Could this have been an even greater loss for them? Absolutely. Typically a customer who has a negative experience will tell their friends and others about it, even more than if they had a positive experience. In my case, I chose to just never return.

Make your business one that doesn't shy away from negative customer feedback and instead chooses to address and resolve issues head-on. Do this and you'll retain that customer in the future. Remember, finding a new customer is a lot more expensive than retaining a current one. See unhappiness as an opportunity for greatness, and focus on solving the issue rather than avoiding it. You will have a far greater customer loyalty by adopting this practice.

ACTION STEPS

1. When you know a customer is unhappy, or even if you suspect they are, take action.

2. Always ask the customer what you could do specifically that would make them happier. This is easier than suggesting options that may not appease them.

3. If their unhappiness is a result of something that you know could happen again—either something wasn't done, or was done incorrectly—is there a way to make sure it will never happen in the future with that customer or others? Fix it.

"Concentrate on your strengths, instead of your weaknesses... on your powers, instead of your problems"

Paul J. Meyer
Success Motivation Institute

WINNING BUSINESS PRACTICE

Double Up on Your Strengths
(Delegate the Rest)

In my early years as a Realtor there was no task that I didn't personally do. As my business developed and I became more successful I learned what I was good at and what I wanted to do more of. I also learned how to delegate tasks that I didn't need to be involved in personally and that didn't maximize my skill set.

As your business grows learn how to train others so you can focus on your strengths. Outsource or delegate any tasks that you can't get to, are weak at, or just don't enjoy.

ACTION STEPS

How can you double up on your strengths?

1. Create a list of the core tasks or roles that you're good at—your strengths.

2. Create another list of tasks or roles that you will either one day delegate, or delegate now.

3. How can you do twice as much of what you're good at? What effect will it have?

"As a property developer, I learned a long time ago to choose your battles wisely and that, unfortunately, compromise is a given."

Kevin McCloud
Designer, Author and TV Host of *Grand Designs*

DEALING WITH CHALLENGES

Choose Your Battles

Every week of your career there will be a moment when you're being bullied or manipulated and you might feel that you have a just cause to fight back. If you're like me then every battle that you engage in you'll want to win. However, you don't need to fight every battle and it won't help you.

In my many interactions with peers and clients where competition is present, I always ask myself if this is a fight that I want to own or is it one I can move past.

One example where I consciously made a decision to put aside my desire to make a sale, was for previous clients who were listing again. Unfortunately, I'd made the original sale when they were a couple and now they were divorcing. We had become friends and one of them quite naturally turned to me to make the sale. As much as I would have loved to have gotten them a great deal and sold that listing, I didn't try to convince the other that I could because I knew in my heart I was too connected. It was the right thing to do to refer another agent and move past this one.

Another time I decided I needed to fight for a listing. I had a previous client who was selling their condo but had an interested buyer in his neighbor and friend. It seemed like an easy sale to the owner and he wanted to sell to his friend, but to me the friend's offer was too low. I knew it was below market price and not in my client's best interest to accept. I kept my emotions cool, to analyze the right thing to do. I fought for the right to have him list it with me and put it on the market quickly, but I had to get creative. The way I negotiated it was, to write up an agreement with a clause that if I couldn't find a much better price, we would sell it to the friend at the price he wanted. I did, of course, find a buyer at a much better price.

Choose your path forward by putting your energy into efforts that will give you only positive results. Don't get sucked into creating or having a battle when it wastes time, money and can put stress on relationships.

ACTION STEPS

Do you have a battle you're about to undertake? Each time you are, use these Actions Steps:

1. First, be clear with yourself by trying to separate your emotions from the moment at hand and your own motivations to make sure you're doing the right thing for the client.

2. Ask yourself if you have the time and energy for this battle and if it will be worth it in the end. In every tricky situation there are many ways forward. Consider whether fighting the battle will negatively affect future relationships.

3. When you decide whether to fight or let it lie, have the comfort of knowing you used your wisdom.

"Buyers decide in the first eight seconds of seeing a home if they're interested in buying it. Get out of your car, walk in their shoes and see what they see within the first eight seconds."

Barbara Corcoran
Real Estate Entrepreneur on *Shark Tank*

STARTING OUT

Presentation! Presentation! Presentation!

Presenting a property well is an art form that you want to master. Far too often, I've seen selling agents show a property and highlight the negatives of it versus the positives without even being aware they were doing it.

I keep seeing Realtors stomp around older, wood-framed houses, further accentuating that it may be noisier than a newer house. Or, crowding the clients in a smaller space and inadvertently revealing the home's size limitations. I often see minor things that obviously need fixing, and would take very little effort to remedy, left undone. I hear Realtors making excuses for things that they don't even know are important to the buyers. All of these behaviors leave an overall negative perception in the buyer's minds.

When I walk into an older wood-frame home, I've learned to literally walk with a light step. You don't need to draw attention to the sound transference of your listing. In all other ways showcase the positives of your listings and minimize the negatives. If you have an older property, for instance, focus on the embedded value it contains for future growth. If you have a small property, don't crowd the buyers. Instead, let them go in each room by themselves. If you have a brand new listing, focus on the lack of maintenance that will be needed and so forth.

ACTION STEPS

1. Always find at least five positive attributes of each listing and present them first. Repeat their merits in different ways.

2. Identify at least five potential negatives and have solutions to them IF they come up.

3. Make sure your listings are well presented physically and make them as impeccable as you can.

4. Practice walking softly and not crowding buyers.

SELF MANAGEMENT

Don't Get Even, Get Better

It's hard for me not to think about wanting to get even when something happens to me or when I experience a situation that bothers me. Time and life experiences have shown me that people do what they do for a reason. The best way to get even is not by getting back at whoever you feel imposed on you, but by focusing on becoming the best version of yourself.

In 2015, I was happy to learn that a friend of mine, who was a public figure, won his court case against a reporter for defamation of character. I was glad he proved himself to be the man I knew he was. Early on in his troubles however, I felt that he was being too passive and should have been more aggressive against the malicious accusations against him.

Little did I know that his choices for dealing with this crisis would effectively illustrate to me the best version of who he was. He didn't need to get even, he just needed to clear his name and show his true character by his actions. Even under tremendous public pressure he walked a path of integrity and came out of it stronger.

Getting even is a long and sad game. An eye for an eye makes the whole world blind and it is exhausting. Understand that things will happen to you and life will go on. Rather than dwell on this, great leaders understand this as a law in life and focus on making themselves stronger so that they're equipped to face these challenges more effectively.

ACTION STEPS

In your business, you too are a leader. You will want to manage yourself so that you're spending your time getting better rather than getting even. Look at all leaders, not just other real estate agents.

1. Be a conscious leader by looking at how other leaders improve themselves. Make a list of three or four things they do that you aren't doing, or could be doing more of.

Be the change you want to make.

WINNING CUSTOMER SERVICE

You Are Always "On"

Everywhere I go in the world of real estate I act as if I'm on camera and my Grandma is watching me. When showing homes I've walked in on couples in intimate moments, found many unmentionables and witnessed interactions that my clients would never want mentioned. I treat each moment with the utmost respect and discretion. I always have my integrity, tact and winning customer service persona "on" as if I stepped onto a stage.

ACTION STEPS

1. Always show up at least five minutes early to everything and tell the client you'll be there early for showings.

2. Knock on the door and do a sweep of the property. Never judge or gossip, just focus on your job to close the deal in your client's best interest.

3. Don't answer the phone or go into a meeting if you're not ready to be "on."

> *"All growth depends upon activity. There is no development physically or intellectually without effort, and effort means work."*

Calvin Coolidge
30th U.S. President

WINNING BUSINESS PRACTICE

Volume Fixes Everything

If I think back to my first year in the business, every detail and dollar seemed important. I was focused on trying to control all the factors that were influencing outcomes, versus focusing on how I could impact outcomes. And, I could impact outcomes by focusing on volume. The volume I'm talking about includes: leads, listings, sales, number of strategic alliances you make, etc. It means, the more volume I did, the more I saw that I was moving forward a lot quicker in life than trying to intimately control the small things and small amounts.

Volume is like the tide of an ocean versus the ripple in a pool. The pool looks big until you meet the ocean. The best way to maximize your growth is to focus on achieving your volume targets. The more volume you create in your business, the more options you'll have.

ACTION STEPS

1. Figure out what result you're aiming for, and work backwards to determine the volume targets needed to

achieve it. Example: You want to make 50 sales this year. If that's the case, how many leads do you need? How many people do you need to talk to? How many buyers? How many listings? Figuring out the volume recipe you need, rather than focusing on how many clients you already have.

2. Start with volume of leads to get to your goals. Determine how many clients converted and how quickly. This will help you more accurately calculate realistic volume targets.

Expanding your volume has the trickle-down effect of consistently growing your business which will help you grow as a Realtor.

DEALING WITH CHALLENGES

Toxic Deals

No matter how hard you try, as you do more deals you'll encounter clients and situations that become toxic. I once obtained an expired listing that was overpriced. Unfortunately, the seller wasn't willing to lower the asking price. However, I felt that I could help him reach his sales objectives and I took on the listing anyway.

Over the next nine months, I listed the property several times, negotiated on six different offers, and eventually made a successful sale. However, once the subjects were removed, the seller's behavior became toxic. He accused me of not looking out for his best interests as he began to get scared about finding a new place. Although I'd been looking out for his best interest the entire time, he began to think that I wasn't on his side.

As we began searching for his new home, our relationship continued to break down and I realized I wasn't going to change his perspective. I wanted nothing more than to fire him and move on. However, I decided to try my best to assist him with his upcoming purchase. Three weeks later he proceeded to buy his new home with a different agent, a result that I saw coming. Yet, in this case, it was clear to me that working for free was a better option than dropping the client and potentially dealing with an unfounded Real Estate Council investigation. Sometimes it may be possible to drop the clients to get out of a toxic situation, but it's always better to avoid those potentially toxic situations in the first place (see Week 38, Choose Your Clients).

ACTION STEPS

Recognize when you're in a difficult spot and consider the following:

1. Clients have different motivations and they often see things from a fear-driven or opportunity-driven perspective. Accept that you may not be able to change their perspective.

2. You always have a choice. Sometimes the best choice is to continue working with a client, even if there is no financial benefit for you, if it will reduce the toxicity of the situation. This can help you move on to close the transaction and stop the issue from expanding.

3. When all is said and done, let it go.

WEEK 11

STARTING OUT

Does Your Car Matter?

I drive a new $30,000 Nissan Rogue and before that I drove a $30,000 Ford Escape. In past years, I've always had nice, normal, smallish SUVs that I keep tidy. Still, from time to time when I'm working with buyer clients, they make a comment that the selling agent has a fancy Mercedes or BMW or other luxury vehicle. Certain clients do think that the type of vehicle an agent drives reflects how successful they are, but I often know that those other agent do one tenth of the volume that I do. It's not bad to have or want a luxury car but ultimately it won't help you be a better agent or sell more.

I do the majority of my business with normal and hardworking folks. I've never lost a client because I drove an entry level SUV. My service and production speaks for itself and I choose to invest my resources in my business so that one day I can buy the car of my dreams. Realistically, though, it may always be a stretch to buy a $70,000 to $125,000 car. If you can get past the idea of client perception of your vehicle, you can be more conservative in your materialistic spending and instead focus your resources on the things that really matter and will help you generate more business.

ACTION STEPS

1. Don't buy a fancy car if you can't afford it, just for image.

2. Speak with your trusted accountant before leasing a new vehicle. There are limitations to the amount of a lease you can write off for tax purposes.

3. If you don't have an accountant—get one. Their advice can help you avoid making costly financial decisions, help you minimize your taxes, and assist you in achieving your desired business growth. Plus the fee you pay them is tax deductible and money well spent.

"Positive thinking is the key to success in business, education, pro football, anything that you can mention. I go out there thinking that I'm going to complete every pass."

Ron "Jaws" Jaworski
Quarterback and ESPN Analyst

SELF MANAGEMENT

Reflect the Positive

As you become a busier and more successful Realtor you will find you will feel less joy from the wins and more sadness about the losses- fix this! In my sixth year I found myself talking with my peers far more about the missed opportunities rather than focusing on much larger (or far greater) number of wins I was achieving. As much as I hate to remember this period, it did happen and it was holding me back. Pretty soon I got sick of listening to myself and took the following actions steps.

ACTION STEPS

1. Once in a while write down all the things that are working well in your business and the successful transactions you've had.

2. Also, write down the lessons you learned from the opportunities that didn't go your way. The missed opportunities are your best friends for getting to the next level.

43

> *"In sales, a referral is the key to the door of resistance."*

Bo Bennett
Businessman and Author of *Year to Success*

WINNING CUSTOMER SERVICE

Not For You? Refer It

I recently lost a client because I was too busy to take the time to determine if I was the right fit for their needs. I was trying to move into an area beyond my expertise. Because I wasn't active in determining who would be the right agent for the task, me or someone else, I lost not only the client but lost the relationship. The relationship is what generates future referrals. I may have permanently tarnished their view of my business and therefore am highly unlikely to get future referrals from them.

ACTION STEPS

1. Be honest with yourself.

2. Make sure that you're able to provide your clients with top-notch service, even if that service is to find someone else who is excellent.

3. Make sure that you have the knowledge, time and drive to ascertain the facts, do the work and achieve your client's goals.

4. Create a great list of referrals who will always make you look good.

Doing a deal poorly has long-term negative impacts that are far greater than the short-term positive cash flow that you receive from the commission check.

WINNING BUSINESS PRACTICE

Know Your Numbers

As a Realtor you start from nothing. Your numbers are neither bad nor good. Once you start to see results, begin to find the value in your results, then frame those numbers and begin to use them in your business. For example, in my first year of business I sold 17 properties and in my sixth year in business I sold 87 properties. In the span of those years, I learned to track my sales results and convert the numbers into palatable statistics. The stats I'm talking about are: days on market, your sell-price-to-list, percentage of sold listings, how many a year versus location and industry peers, etc. Having this data and combining it with a strong understanding of the ebbs and flows of the market, as well as correct positioning is gold. If you know all these numbers and more you can analyze what you can do to improve your business.

The advantage you can leverage in the real estate industry is that most agents have no idea about their numbers. They don't know their average days on market to sell a house, how often they sell above list price, their sold to active ratio, etc, etc. What I've discovered is that I could take any one of my past years in the industry and compile stats that would encourage a client to trust me with their business. As you begin to track your numbers, and know them inside and out, you're going to find that you separate yourself from the competition. Knowing your numbers creates an uneven playing field in your favor!

ACTION STEPS

1. First and foremost, track and analyze your numbers.

2. Once you have the stats, review the results to determine what can be done to improve them or how you can leverage your strengths.

3. Promote your positive stats and how you compare to the competition in your pitch to prospects.

> *"That's the thing about business. Facts and numbers and results actually count. It's not just about words as it is in politics."*

Carly Fiorina
Former CEO of Hewlett Packard

> *"We don't spend our days thinking about Microsoft or trying to get revenge on Microsoft. That's a really negative and backward way, and that's not how I want to live."*

Mitchell Baker
Founder of Mozilla

DEALING WITH CHALLENGES

When You Get "Robbed"

You'll be amazed at the great friendships and relationships you develop in your real estate business. You will also be surprised at some client's lack of moral compass. I recently had a couple who took a very long time to move towards their purchase, steadily asking for my assistance, opinion, care and attention. We wrote a number of offers but nothing came together. Then, one week the property they wanted was sold to another person because they acted too slowly for our market. I feared this could happen and had warned them about this possibility.

Then they went ahead without my knowledge and bought a pre-sale townhouse from a sales office without any representation. I felt "robbed." Part of me would have loved to tell them how poorly I thought of their actions, but I knew better. Instead, I chalked it up to genuine ignorance of the system on their part. And, it really is my duty as a Realtor to inform clients from the beginning about the speed of the market, the openness of communication required, how I get paid, and the scope of my contract to represent their best interests. So, I left it with good will as a lesson learned.

ACTION STEPS

1. Always remember that the business world is small. Whenever you're angry, know that it's the least suitable time to give feedback to clients or colleagues.

2. When you find yourself in emotional situations, remove your personal motivations and feelings and try to look at all the factors at play that created the situation… then tell yourself you'll sleep on it before taking any action.

When I rationally review a situation where my best interests were not met and give myself some time to reflect, I often see with far greater clarity all the hidden factors that resulted in that outcome. Taking this approach often gives us a broader perspective and allows us to see our stumbling blocks, and prevent them in the future. You'll develop the wisdom to recognize that this will blow over and you'll feel happy that you didn't respond in an irrational or dramatic manner.

"If you are not able to manage your distressing emotions, if you can't have empathy and have effective relationships, then no matter how smart you are, you are not going to get very far."

Daniel Goleman
Social Media and Workplace Author

> *"Our relationships with people are formed by small moments - and relationships are crucial in business."*

Tom Rath
Business Consultant and Researcher

STARTING OUT

Meet and Keep Meeting People

Networking is the life blood of your business. Meet with as many people as you can to network, build relationships and grow your database. I recently made the mistake of not continuing to meet with more mortgage brokers, focusing all my financing referral business to three strong lenders. Then one of the lenders had a sudden and dramatic career change and left the business. I'm now missing this connection and the two deals a year on average that this lender generated for me. If I had more lines in the water, more connections, then the impact of losing that one would have been greatly reduced.

ACTION STEPS

1. Schedule one business building meeting each week. Note that this is easy to do when you have lots of time and hard to maintain as you get busy. This is hugely beneficial to your long term success though, so don't forget to do it.

> *"When you show deep empathy toward others, their defensive energy goes down, and positive energy replaces it. That's when you can get more creative in solving problems."*

Stephen Covey
Author of *7 Habits of Highly Effective People*

SELF MANAGEMENT

Just the Facts

Throughout my career I've experienced complicated emotional situations with clients and other agents. Tempers flare and emotions skyrocket because buying and selling real estate is expensive and scary for most people. I learned early on that the best professionals are those who can take control of the situation and manage their emotions.

ACTION STEPS

Whenever you find yourself in a difficult situation, make a commitment to yourself to always be the rational one. Never take an adversarial position. Recognize that the clients aren't involved in the vast number of transactions that you are, yet they're most impacted by the outcome and so naturally can be expected to be the more passionate ones in the situation. When you're dealing with other agents who become agitated or emotional, rely on your three strengths:

1. The facts. If the facts are in your favor, focus on the facts.

2. The Law. If the law is in your favor, focus on the law.

3. Say less and listen more. Don't respond emotionally and don't take the attack personally. Often when someone has gone on a rant they later regret it, so make sure you're the listener and not the talker in this situation.

WINNING CUSTOMER SERVICE

Managing Remorse in Buyers and Sellers

Buying and selling a property can be like an emotional roller-coaster for your clients. You need to prepare yourself and your clients for the natural effects of buyer's remorse and seller's remorse. Personally I've had clients who, upon removing subjects on a purchase or on a sale, regret their decisions. I've had clients who have achieved an amazing deal on their transaction and later decide not to continue working with me because I was focused on the deal and not able to effectively manage their emotional roller-coaster and they felt lost in the transaction. No matter how good the deal is, they often feel remorse, after the papers are signed.

I once had a client who was looking to move from her condo to a detached house. For her, there was a certain romance about living in a house that was strengthened by a new child coming.

I found her an excellent deal on a detached house, which she signed off on. But as the close date approached, she decided she didn't want to go through with it. Suddenly her comfortable, existing apartment was looking like a better fit for her and the romance of a house was gone. I let her know that legally and financially she was obligated to go through with the sale. Since we'd gotten such a good deal, I was sure we could resell quickly at a great profit. She was still balking and clearly afraid but I didn't want her to be heading into a law suit. I had to keep making it clear to her that no matter what she was going to do, move or not move, she was going to come out ahead in this deal.

In the end, she never did move in but she made a 30% profit on a resale. This experience made me acutely aware that buyer/seller remorse is a reality in this business and that it's my job to manage this for everyone's benefit.

ACTION STEPS

1. Get to know your clients and understand who they are. Why are they buying/selling? When you know that, you can figure out ways of helping them through the emotions. Just because you may have generated a terrific transaction for your client doesn't automatically mean they will see it that way.

2. Equally important to ensuring you achieve the best outcome for your clients is to manage their emotions. Make yourself available at all the critical steps and

have the client also "emotionally sign-off" on their critical decisions.

3. To minimize the natural buyers or sellers' remorse, stay in constant contact throughout the process. Handle concerns as they come up. Don't wait for them to fester.

"When I was 18, and entered my family business, I soon realized that it wasn't as easy as I thought. I had to deal with people of my father's generation. Building trust was key to doing business."

Binod Chaudhary
CEO and Founder CG Corp Global, in Forbes 500

WINNING BUSINESS PRACTICE

Building Trust in Your Business Relationships

I had clients who, with a previous Realtor, missed out on their dream of owning a detached house more than once, in a very competitive market. So, they were very anxious when I presented an offer for them in a multiple offer situation to the selling Realtor who was an industry leader. The offer was clean and subject free but not the highest. The seller accepted our offer. Why? I had done several deals prior with the selling Realtor and she trusted me to manage things smoothly. She was able to convey my reputation and deal-closing ability to his client. This made her client confident and happy to work with us.

ACTION STEPS

1. Make sure to foster, grow and maintain a strong industry reputation. There are many examples in this book about acting with integrity and rewarding your referrals to ensure you have an excellent reputation.

Realtors want to look out for their sellers best needs so if you're a Realtor representing a buyer in a competitive environment, it helps to do business with people who trust, respect and like you.

DEALING WITH CHALLENGES

Be a Hero

To err is human. You will make mistakes and the more business you do, the more mistakes you'll make, even with great due diligence. Issues will arise and some will be your own fault and some will not, but they fall back on you.

When things go wrong, even if you're to blame, remember it's an opportunity to save the day and be a hero. Some of my best clients developed from moments of crisis. On the opposite side of the spectrum, I've had some easy deals that went perfect but the client was under-impressed. It went too smoothly and there was no opportunity for me to differentiate myself from the average sales person. Better to embrace the challenges and let your skills shine.

ACTION STEPS

1. Focus on the opportunity to solve a problem and thereby create an amazing experience. Rectify an issue that 90% of other Realtors would simply try to avoid, deflect or deny. Be a hero.

> *"When selling to close friends and family, no matter how cheap you sell to them, they still won't appreciate it."*

Jack Ma
CEO and founder of Alibaba

STARTING OUT

Family and Friends

One of the hardest things to learn as you go forward with your real estate career is that your friends and family don't automatically translate into clients. This is a difficult realization, but it makes sense when you think about it. Typically, you don't mix finances with family or friends and real estate is often the biggest financial decision in most people's lives.

I've experienced the highs of family and friends choosing to work with me and the lows of seeing them choose to work with another more qualified agent at the time. Keep your relationships and your business separate. Remember that the reason they may not work with you is not because they don't trust or love you, but usually it's because they don't think you have the experience yet. Get the experience and they often will become your client next time.

ACTION STEPS

1. When you first get into the industry, communicate with all your friends and family about your exciting new career.

2. Ask them if they already have a Realtor they trust and no matter what the answer, ask them if they're willing to have you stay in touch and receive valuable information from you periodically about their real estate market.

3. First and foremost, make sure to thank each one of your family and friends who choose to work with you, especially when you don't have the experience. These are extra special people.

Family and friends will often say yes to you because of your relationship. This is your advantage over their current Realtor and any other Realtor. This is your window to start showing them your skills, your exceptional customer service and your differentiating features. Over the next few years, you'll be able to show how much you've grown professionally. Combining this reputation with your relationship will eventually make you

their Realtor of choice.

SELF MANAGEMENT

Your Boundaries

With hard work and persistence, almost anyone can do almost anything. However, we all have our strengths and weaknesses. A good Realtor will quickly identify what they want to take on and what's best to refer out to another professional. Early in my career when I had very little business, I took on clients with goals of buying or selling that were outside of my ideal focus. At the time, I was willing to educate myself accordingly to ensure that I offered them great service. Later, as I got busier, I chose to take on less of these transactions if they were out of my core skill set or focus.

You may go outside your boundaries to start, when you're hungry, but it takes discipline and self management to begin only going with your strengths. For example, in 2016, I needed to find a commercial space for another business venture. I smartly referred out my own commercial business to a highly focused and skilled commercial agent to get the job done more effectively and efficiently. Even though I may one day decide to focus more on commercial work, for now I know it's not a boundary I should cross.

ACTION STEPS

1. When an opportunity comes your way, be self-critical and ensure that this is a job that is within your boundaries and skill set.

2. Be selective in your approach and the business that you take on. Don't get bogged down in transactions that you're unfamiliar with and that take your time and energy away from your core focus.

"You don't need a big close, as many sales reps believe. You risk losing your customer when you save all the good stuff for the end. Keep the customer actively involved throughout your presentation, and watch your results improve."

Harvey Mackay
Businessman and author of *Use Your Head to Get Your Foot in the Door*

WINNING CUSTOMER SERVICE

The Customer is NOT Always Right

I had a buyer who could have bought for many years and profited handsomely, but didn't because they were their own worst enemy. This was the type of client who had convinced themselves, and the people around them, that the market was this-or-that or it was on the verge of a crash. This customer ended up associating with like-minded people, and driving away anyone who challenged their thinking. This buyer held his belief so tightly that in the end it cost him time, energy, and a lost opportunity.

From the initial meeting with this buyer, I was clear and honest about my professional opinions backed by facts to counter his assumptions about the market. I told him that he had an opportunity to put the past behind him as a lesson learned. He could start fresh with me, a Realtor that will push back if it's in the client's best interest, even if we disagree.

The result was that I challenged my client many times on assumptions and statements that he made; ideas that would have prevented him from ever buying. Ultimately, he did listen to my guidance and is now a very happy real estate investor.

ACTION STEPS

Multiple times each year a situation occurs in which a client states their opinions as if they're fact. This type of client often comes at you like a steam train and thinks they're right because the people with the counter facts, opinions or thoughts have already moved away from them to get out of the way of the "train."

1. Choose your "steam trains" wisely as they can be very exhausting to work with.

2. Assemble your facts and keep them at hand to refute the ideas your client may have. The client is not always right.

WINNING BUSINESS PRACTICE

Know Your Client

Over months of slowly cultivating an email relationship with a prospect to sell their condo I finally received the opportunity. They wanted to sell. Unfortunately, I didn't bother to get to know my client better and made an error that cost me their business.

The seller had requested that I do research to ascertain the market value of the listing, so I got right on it. Somewhere in the process I looked at a very similar comparable property that I confused as the client's property. It looked like the prospective seller had lived there for a very short time (less than a year). In a follow-up email with my prospective seller I asked them why they were looking to sell so soon after purchasing it. They responded with a simple and short email stating that they had owned the property for 23 years!

My innocent mistake gave the impression that I had not done my research and had certainly not gotten to know the client. The listing opportunity evaporated from just that one email.

ACTION STEPS

1. Always re-read your emails before you send them. If you're sending any key information such as dates, times numbers, dollars or other facts, re-read and re-confirm that your information is correct. There are few things more frustrating than spending a lot of time and energy cultivating a hot prospect, only to send them a mistake which extinguishes the "flames of business."

2. Don't assume you know something. Create a list of key questions to ask all your clients at the beginning, like "How long have you lived at your current home?"

"The knowledge that you have emerged wiser and stronger from setbacks means that you are ever after secure in your ability to survive."

J.K. Rowling
Author of *Harry Potter* and franchise

DEALING with CHALLENGES

Downswings

No matter how long you've been working in the industry, you're going to go through great up-swings and also some down swings. In 2015, I had an amazing year, but the last quarter of the year started with a real down-swing. In a three week period I felt like I was losing more than winning-something I'm not used to. During this time I had several listings come off the market and several listing opportunities go to other agents. I wrote several offers for opportunities that were not reoccurring and came in second too many times!

Instead of panicking I reminded myself that this would pass and I would get back on a good run in no time.

ACTION STEPS

1. Never get so high on the highs that you think the lows will never come. They will come and they will pass and you will learn the art of riding the ups and downs.

2. Find a colleague in the industry you can turn to for advice and input. During the downswings, figure out

what you did well and figure out what you need to improve on. Use your downswing times to learn.

3. See the next lesson about keeping a journal; write down your thoughts on your downswing on a weekly or daily basis as an outlet for your thoughts and emotions.

"The starting point of discovering who you are, your gifts, your talents, your dreams, is being comfortable with yourself. Spend time alone. Write in a journal."

Robin S. Sharma
Speaker and Author *of The Monk Who Sold his Ferrari*

STARTING OUT

Keep a Journal

Keep a journal where you document and analyze your day, your results and the tasks you complete. It will provide you with a document that you can reflect back on. This will give you clarity in the future, give you strength when issues reinvent themselves and it will give you ways of discovering low-level tasks that can be outsourced so that you can focus on higher-level and income generating activities.

ACTION STEPS

1. Buy a Journal
2. Start a journal—if you can't complete daily entries, strive for at least weekly.

"*You will never feel truly satisfied by work until you are satisfied by life.*"

Heather Schuck
The Working Mom Manifesto

SELF MANAGEMENT

Your Health

By the end of a busy year I had let myself get out of physical shape. I gained 25lbs of excess weight and it began to affect my results. I'm not comfortable or built to be 200lbs. My ideal performance body is 175-180lbs. I know that as I get close to my ideal performance weight that my confidence increases, my clothes fit better, my energy level is higher and I feel like a rock-star and all the opposite results occur when I'm not at my ideal weight.

ACTION STEPS

Be honest with yourself about your health. I slowly gained the 25 lbs over a few years and I was on the verge of not fitting into my standard clothing, let-alone my favorite power clothing. We all come in different sizes and styles, but only you know what your ideal shape, size and fitness is that makes you perform at your peak.

1. Have a sustainable health regime that you can stick to, even when things get busy.

2. Know when you're busy you'll have a greater temptation to eat on the run and make bad diet choices. Stay up a few minutes later and pack a lunch and keep healthy snacks in your car.

3. Take care of any other health concerns promptly.

4. Document your goals and find an accountability partner. Make the necessary steps to reach your ideal performance body—it will do a world of good for you, your family and your business success.

"Business is all about the customer: what the customer wants and what they get. Generally, every customer wants a product or service that solves their problem, is worth their money, and is delivered with amazing customer service."

Fabrizio Moreira
Talent Agent, Businessman, Activist

WINNING CUSTOMER SERVICE

Over Service

No single transaction is worth getting in trouble for. A way of avoiding problems and mitigating your risk is to over service your clients. By over servicing your clients, you establish a strong relationship where your clients not only trust you, but also care for you. By over service, I mean stay in touch, do what you promised and beyond what you promised. When you do this, they're less likely to blame you for potential problems and more likely to work with you to find solutions to problems.

ACTION STEPS

1. Create a client service checklist of what you want to accomplish. List the basics and what you want to do to go over and above what other Realtors do. Keep accomplished lists on file as a great document for your confidence and if there is ever an issue.

2. Even if you don't use the checklist every time, periodically review the checklist to remind yourself of the basics and the things you do to go above and beyond.

3. Review your list regularly to see if it needs updating from the lessons you learned.

WINNING BUSINESS PRACTICE

The Monthly SWOT

I find myself more focused and organized when I compose a periodic analysis of my business that organizes my Strengths, Weaknesses, Opportunities and Threats (SWOT). This is a common management tool many larger businesses use and even if you're a solopreneur, you should be doing this kind of analysis too.

Here are some key questions to consider for your SWOT analysis:

- **STRENGTHS** - What has helped you gain the most success to date and is unique to you and your business? These are your strengths.

- **WEAKNESSES** - What has lost you business and opportunities in the past? These are your weaknesses.

- **OPPORTUNITIES** - What conditions or trends are coming up in the market place that you should try to leverage? These are your opportunities.

- **THREATS** - What possible new legislation, possible financial downturns, new competition or other challenges might be coming up and how are you going to plan for them?

ACTION STEPS

1. Early in your career, start a successful habit of creating a monthly SWOT analysis of your business and yourself. When you get really busy, the new objective will be a quarterly SWOT analysis. Establishing this habit will go a long way towards your future success.

DEALING WITH CHALLENGES

Brainstorm Mistakes

The mistakes I've made have helped me learn, grow and prevent future mistakes from reoccurring. Yet, this can only happen when I stop and reflect on my mistakes to figure out what I could have done differently. Sometimes this has to happen quickly and on the fly to be effective so you can get better at doing this efficiently.

ACTION STEPS

1. When you make a mistake or lose money, prevent the loss from increasing and stop the "bleeding." In other words, don't throw good money (or time) after bad. If it isn't working, cut it out right away–don't wait.

2. When you have a moment, take a step back and brainstorm what went wrong. How can you prevent this from happening again? What do you need to do differently now and in the future?

3. Document this process in your journal. Then make sure you practice it going forward.

"What makes a publishing house great? The easy answer is the consistency with which it produces books of value over a lengthy period of time."

Robert Gottlieb
Past Editor-in-chief of **Simon & Schuster**
and **Alfred A. Knopf** publishers

STARTING OUT

Stay Consistent

Only add a new task, habit, employee, investment or cost to your business if you're able to stay consistent with it and continue it for over six months to see the results. Don't fall for the flavor of the week, instead try those new techniques for six months and monitor your results.

One thing I tried and dumped after a number of months was hiring someone to do licensed cold calling. While they were able to generate leads for me, the leads were not the quality I expected or the type of clients I wanted. So, with no good results, I let the person go. To continue would have been a waste of time and money, but I learned what not to do.

One thing I kept after six months was doing weekly task schedules on Sunday nights. It is a habit I continue because it focuses my week ahead, gives me direction and satisfaction.

ACTION STEPS

1. Make small changes to your business and stay consistent with the changes to be able to measure the results.

2. Once you have done something for six months, re-evaluate it and do one of three things:

    a. Stay the course if it's working.

    b. Make slight adjustments to maximize and improve results.

    c. Discontinue it if it's not working, including letting go of someone (for hiring tips see Week 48 - Should I Hire an Assistant?).

SELF MANAGEMENT

Venting

At times, I catch myself venting about an experience or some aspect of my work life, to a peer, a client or to the wrong person. The wrong person would be any client, even a past client, the Realtor you're currently negotiating with, any person in your life who is negative, or anyone you don't completely trust and who can't be a solid sounding board.

To the wrong person venting can come across as disrespectful and unprofessional. The real estate business can be unforgiving and what you say in the heat of the moment can tarnish your reputation.

ACTION STEPS

1. Find friendly Realtors and peers that you can vent your frustrations to. These need to be caring, understanding and trusted peers that will protect your privacy.

2. Hire a business or life coach for venting as well as enforced self analysis.

"Make it right."

Mike Holmes
Contractor, Businessman, TV Host, Philanthropist

WINNING CUSTOMER SERVICE

Make Things Right

Here are some examples of when I had to make things right even when it cost me:

- I offered to sell my assistant's apartment for a flat fee of $1,000 plus her covering costs. Long story short, after a ton of time and money, we sold her apartment. I gifted them the listing costs only to learn after the fact that the office had listed the commission incorrectly and it registered my $1,000 fee as an extra bonus to the buyer's agent. I should have seen this mistake on the MLS system, but I missed it and it cost me an extra $1,050 of my own money to solve the problem. So this went from me doing a favor for a friend to costing me out of pocket, but it was the right thing to do so I did it without trying to hang anyone else for the bill.

- Another example of making things right was when we sent out expired mailers to sellers. Part of the system is a coupon for a $500 gift card, but in order to receive the coupon you need to advise me of it in advance of listing with us. We landed a listing but we continued to send the client further mailers and after the property sold the client brought me the flyer. Technically, they weren't entitled to the $500 as it was after the sale, but in my heart it was the right thing to do and so I honored it and gave them the $500.

- Another example is when my buyer took possession of their home and the washing machine wasn't working correctly. The sellers and the selling agent had no interest in solving the issue. I felt there was long term potential in the client and that the right thing to do was to solve the problem, so I bought my client a new washing machine.

ACTION STEPS

1. Have a core belief in doing the right thing.

2. Do whatever you can to solve problems and make your client happy. This means looking out for their best interests, even if it costs you.

WINNING BUSINESS PRACTICE

Expired Listings

Every single property can be sold. When faced with a challenging listing, it's your job to find the right way of showcasing the property and ultimately the right buyer. In my fifth year in real estate, I began to focus on taking on expired listings. Why? From my experience, most expired listings were unsold, not because the listing agent wasn't doing their job, rather it was simply a result of the seller not being realistic in their expectations. If you can turn that around you can turn that expired listing into gold.

ACTION STEPS

1. When you take listings that may have challenges, analyze them in depth and determine what it would take for you to play the other side and buy the home. This is the honest way to ascertain the market value of a home and then you can develop a plan to maximize the sale price. Remember, it's better to not take on a listing if you can't see an action plan to sell it.

2. You need to be able to effectively communicate your action plan to the client so they're on board and have realistic expectations. Practice keeping it simple for them in a way that most clients can understand. If they can't appreciate it, you may want to move on to another client. This is how you turn expired listings into gold.

DEALING with CHALLENGES

Problems Never Go Away

I can't tell you how often I've listened to someone tell me about a problem that they have and if it were solved life would be easy. The truth is, as you grow and evolve, you realize that problems equally grow and evolve. When you're small, you have small problems. When we grow, the problems also grow, but hopefully our ability to deal with them also grows. I use the daily challenges in my life as opportunities to grow. I try to "frame" my problems into manageable tasks that I know I can accomplish. When a problem seems overwhelming, it just shows me that I have more learning to do so that I can overcome this new challenge.

An example of a small problem is proofreading listings so mistakes don't slip through. You'll always have this small problem but hopefully you have a one-step solution to tackle it. A bigger problem, after you've grown, is your time management when you discover you can no longer do everything yourself. This may require more of a plan than a one-step solution. Time management encompasses bigger and broader problems that you need to break down. These problems never go away either, but you can actively look for better solutions continually.

ACTION STEPS

1. Start to recognize problems as they develop in your life and determine an action plan of steps that will allow you to successfully resolve them bit by bit, day by day.

2. Don't invent the wheel if you don't have to. Look towards bigger people who are successfully tackling bigger problems. You'll find that all your problems have been solved by people before you and if you choose to actively identify and implement their solutions, you can also attain their success.

"Business is a string of seemingly impossible problems looking for solutions. Each problem you solve creates a new barrier to entry for your next competitor."

Jon Oringer
Founder and CEO of Shutterstock

"I think running a business, doing what I've done since 1996, has taught me so many things because I started from just an idea and then had to figure out how to make it, market it, every single thing from soup to nuts on how to get a product done and out there."

Lori Greiner
"Queen of QVC" as seen on *Shark Tank*

STARTING OUT

Fake It Until You Make It

We all start our careers and business with no experience. Why is it that some people go from 0 to 60 so fast and others take a long time or never even get there? The answer is that the pros will learn on the go and work on business and deals with a just-in-time approach. They will surround themselves with experts in the industry and will consistently push themselves beyond their comfort zone. They fake it until they make it. This doesn't mean they misrepresent themselves or their knowledge, it means they learn quickly on the run when an opportunity comes up.

ACTION STEPS

1. Never make up answers for things you don't know or don't have experience with.

2. Develop a group of mentors and peers in your network for you to draw on when you need advice in areas you don't yet have experience with.

3. Develop a habit of giving the right answer after some research instead of the fast (and often wrong) answer. This helps establish your credibility and positions you as a trusted advisor for your clients.

4. Figure out what you need to learn to achieve your short-term and long-term objectives.

"Today I will do what others won't, so tomorrow I can accomplish what others can't"

Jerry Rice
Football Player

SELF MANAGEMENT

Focus and Work Life Balance

I'm fortunate to have a strong support network and a loving, hardworking wife that encouraged me as I found my way as an entrepreneur working 70+ hours a week. Equally, my wife expected that eventually I'd be able to focus my efforts more efficiently and set aside time for the most important things in life. It took me six years of hard work as a Realtor to finally start taking one day a week off. I'm always striving to stay present in the moment and do less, and do it better and with more focus.

Every Sunday morning, I would take my son to gymnastics and then to the pool. Early in my career I had to stop myself from fretting about the other important business issues that were on my mind and calling for my attention. As I got more comfortable with doing this I learned to truly focus on the pleasure I got from having true one-on-one time with my son. As I started to forget about everything else during this Sunday morning ritual, I also saw that clients and colleagues understood and were willing to give me that time and wait for me to respond to their needs later.

ACTION STEPS

1. Work hard to get out of the "starting gate." Put in your hours when you're starting out so that later in your career you'll have the luxury of flexibility.

2. Focus your attention on what you're doing at the moment you are doing it. It helps you be more effective with the task at hand, and allows you to engage more fully with people you're with.

3. If you need more proof of this practice, look at how your mentors and those successful leaders lead their lives. When a world leader is going on a movie date with his spouse or her spouse, do they look at their cell phone about the numerous other urgent matters that are also important? No, they choose to focus on what they are doing. Those other important matters will still be there when the movie ends. Focus on doing more in less time by staying present and acting deliberately.

WINNING CUSTOMER SERVICE

Choose and **Respect Your Clients**

Working with a client is a two-way relationship and a choice. I'm very lucky to have mostly amazing clients and many very good clients. I've had less than five negative clients because I choose my clients carefully. Several times I've chosen to pass on a buyer or not work with a seller because our styles and our beliefs did not align. Sometimes the potential client doesn't respect, value or listen to me. When sellers and buyers are interviewing you, at the same time you must interview them too, because when you start working with them you're choosing to look out for their best interest.

Yes, clients are hard to find and the idea of choosing to not work with a seller or a buyer who will close a deal is a difficult decision. From experience, however, turning down that client now will save you time, headaches, and maybe even money down the road. You have obligations morally and professionally to look out for your client's best interest. If you're not willing to do that you need to remove yourself from the opportunity. As you become more successful in business, these strategic decisions are easier to make and will come more naturally.

ACTION STEPS

1. If you spot "red flags" or incompatibilities when you first meet prospective clients, find a diplomatic way to let them go. Usually this means giving them a referral to better suited agent which is a win-win.

2. After some time in the business, create a profile of the ideal clients you've had the most success with, that were most satisfied with your service and who referred you to others. What were they like? Look for those traits in your next clients. You may even discover a source that will bring you more of the same.

WINNING BUSINESS PRACTICE

Know Your Primary Elements

Make sure that you pay attention to your most valuable assets in the appropriate order. I've lost several opportunities/clients/leads by not recognizing who they were and at what stage they were at. When you know these primary elements, you can apply your attention accordingly to ensure that the most important people or tasks are served first. The action steps below will help you determine these primary elements and how to effectively analyze and prioritize your clients.

ACTION STEPS

1. Divide your business contacts into four key groups:

   a.) **Platinum** are your ambassadors and supporters who use you, refer you, and promote you consistently.

   b.) **Gold** are your transactional clients, who are doing a deal within the next 3-6 months, or are referring you business in the next 3-6 months.

       c.) **Silver** are your past database of clients or referrals. Your goal is to retain 75% of them for the long term.

       d.) **Bronze** are your leads. Keep in mind that it takes a ton of bronze to equal an ounce of gold or a pound of silver, so focus your attention accordingly.

2.) In busy moments make sure your Platinums get attention first, Golds next, and so on. This doesn't mean you ignore your Bronzes, just delegate and prioritize them in a way they will never know that they're not getting great service.

"I talk a lot about taking risks, and then I follow that up very quickly by saying, 'Take prudent risks.'"

Irene Rosenfeld
CEO of Mondelez International

DEALING WITH CHALLENGES

Take Risks but Don't Gamble

Making marketing decisions is a challenge you'll be constantly dealing with. Easy business results or easy money without hard work and strategic marketing doesn't exist. A marketing *risk* is investing in a new method, marketing system or strategy to generate business and achieve positive results. A marketing *gamble* is spending money based on overly optimistic projections or methods that seem far too easy or sound too good to be true. A gambler takes positions that they are not prepared to cover if it becomes negative, whereas risk-takers don't like losing but will take a position that they can cover and that gives them results or teachable moments.

ACTION STEPS

1. Know your numbers when it comes to marketing. Know what the costs are versus the expected

results. Make sure you track and measure the
results.

2. Use your journal to reflect on what worked and
    what you would do better before renewing or
    expanding a marketing strategy.

3. Be wary of exaggerated results and instead
    identify the few things that work best for you
    and your business.

STARTING OUT

Always Pay Your Referrals Promptly

As you grow your business and grow your Realtor referral network, you'll discover that you can add value to your clients and friends by connecting them with Realtors in areas you don't service. If you do a great job you'll also receive referrals.

Referrals are little nuggets of gold as they often lead you to a great client. Always pay your referral fees promptly and with a smile. I used to send commercial referrals to an agent and we had agreed to a standard referral agreement. One of the referrals I sent her took a lot more time and energy than she expected. When she followed up with me after the deal went firm, she suggested that she send me a gift basket instead of paying the referral fee. I was flabbergasted and lost respect for that agent because she didn't want to honor the original agreement.

Not only did I make her pay my earned referral, I ceased to send her any other referrals. Blaming me for her negative experience was very short-sighted and cost her a vast amount of referral business. She reminded me how an agent might feel if I didn't fully honor my agreements.

ACTION STEPS

1. Over service any referrals you receive as you now have two clients to impress and two opportunities to pursue: both the buyer or seller and the person who sent you the business.

2. Under promise and over deliver. I always pay a bit higher referral commission than is typical to distinguish myself from other agents that offer similar service.

3. Make your fellow Realtor feel like a rock star. Any time I drop off keys or leave something behind for a Realtor, I leave them with a lotto ticket or a chocolate bar. These small gestures and minimal investments from me have generated extra opportunities on many occasions.

SELF MANAGEMENT

Accountability not Envy

Why it is that one person can be born into a poor family and raised with limited resources yet make great strides, while another person is raised with wealth and can lose that wealth within one generation? I take great comfort in knowing that some people may achieve more success with the same opportunities I've had, while others may achieve less. This knowledge does two things for me. First, it makes me motivated and inspired when I see amazing achievements by others. Second, it keeps me accountable for both my future achievements and my shortcomings.

Realtors have a tendency to look at their peers doing great deals and instead of becoming motivated they ask *why them and not me?* Choose a different way. Don't get jealous, get motivated.

ACTION STEPS

1. Be accountable. If you have a bad habit of being envious of others success, stop and transform it into self-reflection.

2. Understand that you control your future. Choose to know that others success comes from hard work and luck, BUT luck is created by hard work and you can do the same.

"The keys to brand success are self-definition, transparency, authenticity and accountability."

Simon Mainwaring
Brand and Social Media Marketing
Consultant

WINNING CUSTOMER SERVICE

Only Ambassadors and Supporters

My database grows slowly, but in 2015 I generated over 85 transactions with a database of slightly over 200 people. My goal is to focus my attention on ambassadors and supporters (my Platinums from week 39). Yet, I only had 15 ambassadors in my database. Ambassadors are people who generate at least one transaction each per year and supporters generate one transaction every two years on average The point is, you can do great business with a relatively small database if they're the right people.

ACTION STEPS

1. Review your database quarterly. To be in my database you have to be:

   - A current ambassador

   - A current supporter

   - A valuable service provider (i.e....lawyer, notary, etc.)

- A referral Realtor

- A current or past client

- A lead or a prospect

2. Remove anyone from your DB that doesn't fit into any of these categories so you can better focus on the ones that do.

"In marketing I've seen only one strategy that can't miss - and that is to market to your best customers first, your best prospects second and the rest of the world last."

John Romero
Video Designer and Entrepreneur

WINNING BUSINESS PRACTICE

How is the Client Base Evolving?

Years five and six of my real estate business saw a lot of my clients selling their apartments to accommodate growing families and to capitalize on the increasingly valuable Vancouver property market and move to the suburbs. As a result, many of my original clients were moving beyond my 25 minute service area, and into areas that are beyond my core expertise. Many of my original core clients, who had been instrumental in my early years and who had not only bought their homes with me but referred me to their friends and family, were beginning to use other agents that specialized in their new purchase area.

It took me longer than I would have liked to figure out what was happening, but once I did, I put some action steps into place in order to find out how many were likely to be moving based on their original purchase dates and other factors.

ACTION STEPS

1. Recognize the possibilities of client migration. It took me too long to see it and many Realtors never do. As a result, they

may lose control of their client base and see it slowly shrink without taking timely action to prevent it.

2. Identify what factors are changing. Why is your client selling with you and then potentially buying with another agent? The truth is likely that you're not the industry expert for the new purchase. Ask yourself whether you want to service them for another purchase or if it makes more sense to refer them out?

3. If you choose to work with them for one more transaction, you need to be willing to do the extra homework so that you can effectively compete with the leading Realtors in that new area. You need to over-service your client and show them your knowledge so that you will maintain the relationship.

4. If continuing to service is undesirable or unrealistic, you need to take control by referring them out to one of the great competing agents in that market. By referring them out, you're going to receive a referral commission and you're going to foster a Realtor referral relationship with that new agent. Most importantly, you're going to transition your client in a positive fashion to another industry peer. In this way you stay involved in the process

since you're actively making the decision to step away and you're leaving the door open in case your client decides to move back into your area of specialty. In contrast, if you don't refer them out, you will likely lose your current client to another agent and your client will feel awkward and will likely just stop communicating with you. All round it would be a lost opportunity and a sad way
to end a relationship.

> *"Fighting means you could lose. Bullying means you can't. A bully wants to beat somebody; he doesn't want to fight somebody."*
>
> **Andrew Vachss**
> Bullying Expert

DEALING WITH CHALLENGES

How to Deal with a Bully

First and foremost, choose never to be a bully. To succeed in business though, you need to learn how to deal with bullies when you encounter them. I've a great reputation because I take it seriously and work hard to develop and maintain my good standing. Even so, I still come across bullies in the market place who are over-grown agents with market dominance. They have become bullies due to their insecurities and their need to stay on top.

I clearly remember a very successful agent tearing a strip off of me because they thought I stole their client. In fact, that client was a friend of mine and we had previously worked together. It took every drop of self-restraint I had not to explode back against that agent to defend myself against the false accusation. He was a foul-mouthed bully and over time I learned that this agent had a history of bullying others and getting away with it because he had market dominance.

I avoid working with these type of agents, but when I've to, it reminds me to be more gracious, patient and earn a better reputation. How do you deal with a bully? Keep calm and carry on. Work on your own reputation.

ACTION STEPS

1. Listen twice as much as you talk.

2. Before you react to a bully, take a breath and ask yourself how you would respond tomorrow.

3. Don't engage. Instead, listen and respond patiently.

4. Continue to establish your positive industry reputation.

5. Work hard and never forget. When opportunities appear where you have a choice to either work with a past bully or not, your memory will likely lose *them* an opportunity.

STARTING OUT

What's Your Driving Motivation?

My family motivates, drives and supports me to be a better man/father/businessman/human being. I went into my real estate business with a humble approach, a good amount of fear and a great amount of motivation to generate results to support my family. As a result, I came up with a goal of generating at least one transaction each month—I never cared if it was a small or big transaction—I just wanted to generate business.

As a result, at the time of writing this book, I can count on one hand the number of times I've gone a month without at least one transaction.

ACTION STEPS

1. Determine and discover your driving motivation. Why are you in this business?

2. Make sure that your driving motivation excites and motivates you— if it doesn't, then it's not your driving motivation.

3. Create a list of action items that you need to complete in order to achieve the results that fulfill your driving motivation.

4. Create a list of daily tasks that done, consistently and diligently, will fulfill your action items.

"If we were motivated by money, we would have sold the company a long time ago and ended up on a beach."

Larry Page
Founder of Google

SELF MANAGEMENT

Don't Sell Your Own Home

When it's time for you to sell your own property, please have another Realtor who has an arms-length relationship with you create your current market analysis, as well as take over your pricing and your negotiations.

I've shown and tried to negotiate on three properties that a Realtor owned and their pricing and valuations were CRAZY! Realtors can be the worst clients when it comes to selling akin to doctors being the worst patients. Too much knowledge gets in the way of a down to earth perspective. Price your home properly and it will sell—otherwise don't list your own home as it wastes everyone's time.

ACTION STEPS

1. When you're selling your property, ask yourself what makes a great selling client to you. Then, take the steps to become one. It likely is a person who wants the most for their property,

but looks realistically at market results of recent solds, expireds and actives that are your competition.

2. Take the opportunity to hire another Realtor that isn't emotionally connected and have them direct, guide and advise you towards a successful sale.

WINNING CUSTOMER SERVICE

Should I Hire an Assistant?

Great service costs money. I can vividly remember hiring my first assistant and being so worried about the additional cost this role would add to my business. As I become more comfortable and successful, I'm always excited to hire team members as it means that I'm investing in my business. I choose to invest in people who generate results, make sure my service standards stay high, and give me leverage within three months time. I never invest more than three months into a team member if I don't see the results.

Examples of quantifiable results include: a significant increase in listings, an increase in leads and an increase in closings. I look to see an increase in revenues that at least cover their salary with the ultimate goal of seeing an overall increase in revenues of up to 5x their salary. I also expect to see them demonstrating organizational skills, learning well, making improvements, and receiving positive feedback from clients and associates.

ACTION STEPS

1. It doesn't matter if it's your first year in the business or your 15th year, the time to hire your first assistant is when you either generate over 35 transactions a year, or when you set the goal and decide to generate over 35 transactions a year. Less than 35 transactions is a full time job that a hard working agent can cover, while generating over 35 transactions (or setting the goal to), requires assistance and investment beyond what the average Realtor can do effectively by themselves.

2. Hiring errors can be costly. Spend more energy up front. Figuring out what the right fit is for you. Ask for referrals from others in the business and get their advice on what has helped them the most in finding, hiring, and retaining a strong assistant. You could use a temp agency if you're not sure how to hire as this allows you to keep trying different people until you find the right fit. This can be an expensive route to take, though, as temp agencies typically charge more and if you offer one of their recruits a permanent job you have to pay the temp agency a fee. Another option to boost your own hiring skills would be to take online courses on how to hire.

3. Interview final candidates a few times before hiring (whether by phone, video chat or in person), and then check references.

"It's hard sometimes to take a step back and realize what's happened because you're always trying to move forward. You're always looking at the next..."

Alexander Wang
Fashion Designer, Entrepreneur

WINNING BUSINESS PRACTICE

Take a Step Back

We typically tell ourselves to create an annual business plan or come up with a new set of personal goals each New Year. I try and create a fluid business plan at the beginning of each year that I work from and turn it into a top priorities document. I find that the best plans that I've created are the ones that never seem to be quite complete— plans that you constantly look back to and work from.

ACTION STEPS

1. Create a plan for your business and personal life today. No matter what part of the year you're in, create a plan from now until the end of the year.

2. Come early December, set a goal of creating a business plan for the following year by December 31st. Once complete, carry that plan with you.

3. Block out two half-hour windows each month to review your business plan going forward. You'll notice that there are things from your plan that have become more important and there are things that have never gone anywhere or have evaporated. This is all normal and effective—a business and life plan is a living document that changes and evolves as your priorities and needs change.

DEALING with CHALLENGES

Burn Me Once...

The old saying, *"Fool me once, shame on you. Fool me twice, shame on me,"* also applies in your business. It is important to avoid time leeches and negative contacts that pull you away from providing the best service to your other clients. A core skill as a professional is to know when to remove a contact from your database—especially a contact that burns you. I've spent far too much time working for and trying to help people who are not loyal to me, clients who don't value my time and energy and end up "burning" me.

You may ask, should I tell them how they have wasted my time and energy? The answer is "no." It is better to take the high road and instead focus your time, energy and passion towards the clients you have that are loyal to you, respect your time, and value your expertise.

ACTION STEPS

1. Whenever you get burned by a client or an associate, take some time, debrief and reflect on what happened. Ask

yourself if you could have done something to alter the outcome or if this was out of your control.

2. Then, make a decision whether this is someone who you are willing to invest further energy in or if it's time to bring the relationship to a close.

"Plan for what is difficult when it is easy, what is great when it is small."

Sun Tzu
The Art of War

STARTING OUT

Plan for Better Years

Great agents don't have roller coaster years. They tend to have a business that produces consistent and measureable results that grow year over year. Focus on building a strong foundation in your business to support the targets you want to reach. Good agents succeed in typical markets while great agents succeed in any market, including the most difficult ones. The difference lies in the great agents' constant focus on making each year better than the last.

Create that marketing plan based on what is working and what didn't. Do your research. Review the past numbers and forecast some numbers for next year. In other words, don't just coast or play wait and see, plan for more growth.

ACTION STEPS

1. Appreciate your current success.
2. Learn from your mistakes.
3. Forecast future trends.
4. Create a business plan to do more business next year.

"It's important for me to show my children the richness of life and be a role model. I find that my organizational and management skills are tested more at home than at work!"

Susan Wojcicki
CEO of YouTube

SELF MANAGEMENT

Life Time Management

I was in my mid-thirties before I began to see how delicate and special life is. If we are lucky, we still have many years of joy ahead in our life; however, one never knows when it might all end. Part of the "human condition" is the longing for balance between work and life.

Everyone knows that on their death beds there are very few people who wish they spent more time working. The regrets at death are usually of wishing to have done more: spent more time with family, laughed more with friends and gone on more adventures rather than having worked more hours. However, all-play-all-day will likely not lead to a happy and balanced life either. I personally have made a conscious choice to challenge myself to work hard but also to enjoy the moment I'm in as much as I can. I do this while building a life and wealth that gives me and my family options of what we want to do by the time I'm 50.

This choice has meant that I worked hard from an early age. I started working on a strawberry farm while I was in elementary school and have been working ever since. It was a decision I made that has allowed me to enjoy a happy and financially stable life by my mid-thirties, and be on a path to a financially secure position by my 50's. I made my choice early, but it's not too late to adjust your path.

ACTION STEPS

1. Recognize that you have a limited amount of time on this earth. Each action and decision that you make, or lack thereof, will have a cause and effect. Be deliberate in how you choose to spend your time.

2. Become the person that is actively making decisions and choices in your life, instead of letting life dictate for you. Become self-accountable and appreciate what you have while knowing what you can do to achieve more in your life.

Moving On Up
- Conclusions -

When people buy real estate, they generally see themselves as moving up in the world. When you start a business in real estate, by the end of your first year, you may know if you have the potential to move on up, or you may feel like you want to move onto something else. However, if you are truly using winning business practices, providing exceptional customer service, developing strong self management and dealing with all your challenges as gracefully and as intelligently as you can, then you will have no doubt that you are moving on up.

Please use this book not as a one-time read, but as a regular reminder that you can achieve the results you want no matter what the market is doing.

If you enjoyed this book, I would appreciate you reviewing it on Amazon and letting other agents, or potential agents, know of its value. If you have achieved positive results due to some of my tips or have other feedback, please drop me a line at my web site: RolandKym.com

About the Author

Roland Kym is an award-winning Realtor who is consistently in the top two percent of all Vancouver Realtors. He is passionate about real estate and helping his clients navigate the Vancouver markets.

Roland lives in Vancouver with his wife and three children. They are often outdoors and can be found enjoying the city, mountains and ocean.

You may contact Roland at RolandKym.com or at 604-970-0393.

Made in the USA
Columbia, SC
20 August 2018